IF GOD IS GOD

IF GOD IS GOD

Conversations on Faith, Doubt, Freedom, and Love

RICHARD EDWIN KOENIG

CONCORDIA PUBLISHING HOUSE
SAINT LOUIS   LONDON

232.2

Concordia Publishing House, St. Louis, Missouri
Concordia Publishing House Ltd., London, E. C. 1
© 1969 Concordia Publishing House
Library of Congress Catalog Card No. 77-89878

MANUFACTURED IN THE UNITED STATES OF AMERICA

Contents

Preface   7
1. Do We Need God?   9
2. Thinking About Faith   23
3. The Agony of Doubt   37
4. The Silence of God   53
5. The Way to Christ   69
6. The New Freedom and the Holy Spirit   83
   Notes   97

Preface

ON MY WAY TO VISIT a student at Amherst College, I paused to read a legend tacked to a dormitory door: "The most important contribution of Protestantism is its conclusive proof that God is a bore." H. L. Mencken was the source of the quote, but it is noteworthy that the present generation of students still appropriates the remark as its own. Conversation with college students quickly confirms the suspicion that a majority of young adults entertain serious reservations about the historic faith and hold enthusiasm for institutional religion definitely under control.

Despite skepticism and disenchantment, interest in religion (theology!) is at an all-time high among college students. Those institutions offering credit courses in religion report record enrollments. The paradox of the disappearing chapel and the rise of departments of religion is one of the more interesting phenomena of the posteverything generation. And theological discussions are just as widely carried on outside the classroom. The setting is certain to be informal, the appearance of the participants in miniskirts, boots, beards, and blue jeans a bit startling, but the exchanges are as serious and intelligent as any in previous eras.

This book grew out of conversations with college students in the five-college area of western Massachusetts. It does not include all the themes that keep recurring, but the topics treated are some that surface most frequently. While the chapters are chiefly exposition, I hope the hidden dialog that informs every paragraph is apparent.

My appreciation for the opportunity to converse with those who state their concerns so honestly and intelligently is undisguised. Student probing has been a principal stimulus to my personal theological reflection.

This book assumes both the truth of the historic faith and the necessity to bring it into touch with the questions and sensibilities of today's young adults. Such considerations are reflected in the choice of language. Wherever possible, I have tried to avoid technical theological terminology and use the words and phrases actually employed by young adults when they discuss religious themes. In Chapter 5, for example, theologians would speak of Christ's "deity." I use the word "divinity," since that is the term I have heard often in my conversations with students.

No one writing a book of this type should fool himself into believing that he has provided "answers" for everyone else. My hope is that the book will encourage individuals and groups to develop their own theological approaches to the questions raised. It would be gratifying to learn that the book also succeeded in demonstrating that God is not a bore.

My thanks go to Rev. Gilbert Doan for his critical reading and valuable suggestions, and to Mrs. Jongmo Rhee, a gracious Korean friend, for typing the manuscript.

1
DO WE
NEED GOD?

Do we need God? The answer seemed obvious to most church people in previous generations. Man lived in a world governed by forces beyond his control. He was the victim of evils against which he could do very little. Life was harsh and brutal. Back in runic times the old Norwegians believed a witch was behind the deadly plague that periodically descended on their land. When she went through the village with her rake, only a few would die, but when she swept with her broom, everyone died. Against such forces God was man's sole help. Without Him man was helpless and alone in a dark and evil world.

The Medieval View

In circumstances like this few had to be shown their need for God. The church reassured men that God was present to help, and men believed. This was, of course, no gimmick to gain control of the masses but something the church itself devoutly believed. Convinced of its need, the population of most of Europe rejoiced that in the church it could find God as Refuge and Strength. Churches and cathedrals erected by Christians of the Age of Faith are an impressive and enduring witness to the intensity of their devotion. To be sure, there were always some who lived frivolously, but it was assumed that life would soon teach them the error of their ways. Only the most hardened could refuse to heed the lesson taught in the frequent tolling of the village bell.

The Modern View

The situation in which we live and work in 20th-century America is drastically different.

One by one the places where the Age of Faith felt God was needed have been filled with the achievements and explanations of men of science. Modern man does not call on God to control the plague anymore. He knows about rodent control and sanitation, and if people become ill, he uses antibiotics. God is not regarded as the force that keeps the planets in their orbits. Newton's laws of motion suffice without Newton's God. Frequently God is not even considered necessary to explain how the world came to be. Thinkers are seriously advancing the idea of a continuous creation. Modern culture is characterized by Laplace's famous retort to Napoleon. When the great astronomer put forth his cosmological theory that made no mention of God, the emperor inquired about the omission. "I have no need," Laplace is reported to have said, "for that hypothesis." Since Laplace's day, the need for "that hypothesis" seems to have diminished even more.

Many of my college friends cannot see where God "fits in" any longer. If one of them is sick, he goes to a doctor or surgeon. If he is concerned about the world situation, he hopes the United Nations will work out a solution, whether the crisis is in the Middle East or Central Europe. If there is danger of an economic recession, he looks to Congress or some government agency to get the economy moving again. As far as the beginning or the end of the world is concerned, he couldn't care less. At the moment—and the moment is what counts for my friends of the "now" generation—he is in good shape. His competency allows him to look forward to the future in almost a matter-of-fact way. Life has its ups and downs perhaps, but basically it's fun — even without God.

Faced with a culture that believes God to be unnecessary for human life, some Christians have responded by trying to prove that men must still recognize His necessity today. Some have attempted to make my happy college friends and others realize that they are terribly frightened without God and need Him desperately. Forced on the defensive the church has sometimes been led to play down the achievements of the men of science and scoff at advances in technology. Some Christians believe that for God to stay in business man needs to be convinced that he is miserable without Him even when he really does not feel this way.

But no matter how strongly the church insists that man needs God to secure his life or to explain the mysteries of the cosmos, the majority of people either ignore what is said or remain unconvinced. Scientific knowledge and technological power make it difficult for church people, especially younger members, to see their need for God. With their phone beside them and the numbers of the doctor, the police, the fire department easily available, they hardly "fear the terror of the night, nor the arrow that flies by day, nor the pestilence that stalks in darkness, nor the destruction that wastes at noonday." God is not felt to be the only or even the first line of defense, no matter how devout the Christian may be. Nor do modern Christians conceive of God as a solution to unsolved problems in physics or astronomy. Scientific progress seems to have eliminated the need for God, a development that poses serious problems for Christian faith.

Now, God is still the Creator and Preserver of man and the universe. I could not be a Christian and deny this. Man's relationship to God has not changed since the beginning. What has changed is the way he *senses* that relationship. At certain times desperate circumstances make a person feel his need for and dependence on God in a simple, direct way. Many Christians have had such experiences, and every Christian recognizes the limits of his resources. But often our life seems secure and unthreatened. We have nothing special to worry about at the moment. When this is the case, it is grotesque to *make* ourselves feel terrified and afraid in order that God might have something to do. God is for the strong, the competent, the secure and successful as well as for those in the narrows of life. And He is for those whom even the narrows of life do not make afraid.

The "Death of God"

In some important ways Christians today have to live in and with a world that goes about its business *as if* God is not necessary for man. This was one of the things the "death of God" movement of the 1960s tried to call to our attention. Using the slogan made popular by the 19th-century German philosopher, Friedrich Nietzsche, "death of God" thinkers emphasized that "today only the reality of the world, in all its immediacy and immanence, provides man with a context for possible self-understanding," that "modern man lives in a world of immanence." [1] This is what Nietzsche had prophesied would happen. Nietzsche held that modern man, with his advances in science and technology, had made the God of the medieval world view obsolete. There was a time, argued Nietzsche, when "God" was a necessary presupposition to all that was thought and done. But that time, he said, was over. Mankind's progress had made "God" dispensable. Poetically stated, man had "killed" God, who in reality was nothing more than an idea dreamed up in the childhood of the race. Nietzsche thought it was good riddance.

> The concept "God" was invented as the counter-concept to life — everything harmful, poisonous, slanderous, and all deadly hostility to life, all bound together in one horrible unity.[2]

The purpose of Nietzsche's preachments was to awaken European man to what had happened and make him realize the consequences of his advances in thought, art, science, and culture.

"Death of God" therefore is shorthand for a cultural development of immense importance. The phrase points not only to the fact that God no longer exercises any automatic hold on or fascination for modern man but that man's whole way of looking at the world has changed since the Middle Ages. It has become "secularized" and this-worldly. Man is now the measure of all things. When thinkers use "death of God," they do not always mean to deny God's reality, although it must be admitted that in the case of some this seems to be what is intended. What Christian thinkers are referring to when they employ the phrase is the transformation from the medieval world view to the modern outlook described. Contemporary theologians sense that Christian faith, centering as it does in the living God, faces unprecedented problems in developing a style of life for a culture that seems to erase the very Center of that faith. In a secularized world God-talk seems pointless.

Dietrich Bonhoeffer

Among the first to understand the implications of the "death of God" for Christians was the German Lutheran theologian Dietrich Bonhoeffer, who spoke about the shift from the medieval to the modern world view as the world's "coming of age." Bonhoeffer thought it was good that the "God" of the medieval world view had "died." Why? Because "religious people speak of God when human perception is (often just from laziness) at an end or human resources fail: it is really always their *Deus ex machina* they call to their aid, either for the so-called solving of insoluble problems or as support in human failure—always, that is to say, helping out human weakness or on the borders of human existence." [3] What Bonhoeffer wanted to do was to "speak of God not on the borders of human life but at its centre, not in weakness but in strength, not therefore in man's suffering and death but in his life and prosperity." [4] It is no wonder that Bonhoeffer continues to be one of the most powerful theological influences of our day.

Bonhoeffer's view means that the collapse of the medieval notion of God, so often viewed with alarm by Christians, can actually work to the advantage of genuine religion. None of us has much respect for a person who believes in God only because he is afraid. If I believe in God only because He is the One who helps me in time of trouble, protects me, and saves me from harm, I have reduced the God of majesty to something comic. It would be like saying that the

15

entire United States Air Force with all its Strategic Air Command bombers and nuclear capability exists solely to keep little me safe from harm. If God is believed in chiefly because of what He does for man to make his life secure, then, when the heat is off, man can dispense with God like a worn-out Band-Aid. This is exactly what happens when people relate to God in this fashion. There are no atheists in the foxholes, but there are plenty down on the golf course.

The Point of Contact

If as men of the 20th century we no longer feel we need God for security or to fill the gaps in our thinking or, more precisely, if explanation and security are not the principal reasons we seek Him, why do we recognize Him at all? To put it bluntly, why bother?

The answer is simple. We relate ourselves to God because He is, because He is the fundamental Reality in our lives, because we could not escape Him if we tried. As the psalmist says:

> Whither shall I go from Thy Spirit? Or whither shall I flee from Thy presence? If I ascend to heaven, Thou art there! If I make my bed in Sheol, Thou art there! If I take the wings of the morning and dwell in the uttermost parts of the sea, even there Thy hand shall lead me, and Thy right hand shall hold me. (Ps. 139:7-10 RSV)

The God of the Bible is a God far different from the Cosmic Lever-Puller or the Great Magician of many people's imaginations. He is more than the Giant Protector or the end product of a chain of reasoning. One of the most ill founded of charges against high religion is that the God it serves developed as a "crutch" for people's insecurity. As Martin Buber says:

> The prophets of Israel have never announced a God upon whom their hearers' striving for security reckoned. They have always aimed to shatter all security and to proclaim in the opened abyss of the final insecurity the unwished-for God who demands that His human creatures become real, they become human, and confounds all who imagine that they can take refuge in the certainty that the temple of God is in their midst.[5]

The Biblical God is a God who asks for recognition before any benefit or advantage is announced. The First Commandment does not say: "Please believe in Me, because if you do, you will be healthy, happy, and wise." Rather it announces the presence of Another, whom man is bound to recognize. God is the One in whom, says the Bible, "we live and move and have our being." He is "above all and through all and in all." The mystery of our existence is enclosed by the mystery of God.

It is life itself, therefore, that teaches us to relate ourselves to God on a basis other than one entirely dictated by our real or imagined needs. It is not just a part of life or some particular experience that leads to this new awareness of God, but the totality of life in all its richness and variety, the universe in all its awesome infinity, the mystery of our own selves, that speak God's realness to us. Once that realness is recognized, God is seen not as One who merely fills the gaps in man's thinking or makes up for man's inability to do things. God is the Source of life, its Center, and its Fulfiller. God is in all of life and is encountered everywhere in men's experience.

The Atheist Reply

Despite the Bible's witness to the realness of God, many still insist that there is no God. The origins of modern atheism are complex, but very often the God-deniers operate with the medieval notion that God is the last piece of a mental jigsaw puzzle, the last link in a line of reasoning, or the "answer" to a particular need or problem man may have. The atheist, therefore, is often denying not the Biblical God who embraces more than man's needs but an idol of his own imagination. What gives modern atheism power, as we noted above, is the conviction that there really is no point in bothering with God. Life seems complete in itself. It is a joy to observe the world, to grow up, to dance and laugh and sing. It is fun to establish a home, rear a family, become an artist, architect, salesman, engineer. It is exhilarating to be good at something: carpentry, water-skiing, painting, accounting. Life for many has abundant built-in rewards and satisfactions. When things are going well, just to be is a joy. It is hard to imagine anything better. God seems to get in the way of people who want to taste life in its fullness and avoid pondering mysteries.

It is for this reason that many younger people (and older people too!) put their religion aside or look on it with suspicion. There are few doctrinaire atheists in comparison with those who simply have detached themselves from Christianity because it seems dull and oppressive. When the average person thinks of God, he often has the vague impression of a Being who is watching and keeping score, checking on him to see whether he is being good. Nietzsche's idea appeals to them: God is the counterconcept to life. Everything that is worthwhile, everything that is to be enjoyed, so it seems, is made suspect when God enters the scene. As Emperor Julian the Apostate is reported to have said in his dying moments, "Thou hast conquered, O Galilean, and the world has grown grey at Thy breath."

It must be admitted that there have been Christians who provided a great deal of encouragement for the idea of a joyless God. The memory of what is thought to be the Puritan experience is still alive in the American mind. Even today some Christians seem to be afraid of life and come dangerously close to manifesting a hatred of its substance. They have little appreciation for sex and beauty, food and drink, fun and pleasure, the power to create and invent, for man and his achievements. There is a type of Christian piety that indulges in a depreciation of this world ("Earth is a desert drear") and looks down on God's creation. There are good reasons for such a stance, of course, for life contains a tragic center and always has to reckon with the possibility of the demonic. But that fact has misled some Christians into an apparent denial of life itself.

Life Abundant

It cannot be said forcefully enough that the Biblical God is on the side of life, not against it; that He enters human life not to destroy but to establish it. The Creator in Genesis terms His creation "very good." In Jesus Christ He takes on flesh and blood in this world, the world He made and in which humans dwell. Faith in God, therefore, will lead the believer to participate

19

in life with joy rather than flee or deny it. To be is not only a joy; it is actually holy, for existence comes from God, the Author of all life. The sacred and the secular are not two realms divided by some kind of Berlin wall. It is all God's world, which means that the God who made it can be glorified in the enjoyment of a steak as well as the singing of a hymn. Jesus Christ said that He came that men might have life and have it more abundantly. At the very least, this great saying expresses God's intention to complete, not abolish, to perfect, not extinguish, human life. His breath does *not* make pale the earth.

Where God "fits in" to human life is at the point where man is fully conscious of the greatness and beauty of the gift of life and begins to search for that which is uniquely human. To be a man is to exercise the distinctly human characteristics of love and compassion — in Biblical terms, righteousness. The men of the Bible hear God's voice as the demand for righteousness. They feel His presence in the pressure to do justly, love mercy, and walk humbly with Him. No man is completely devoid of such experiences, even though he may apprehend them dimly. It is here that the real need for God is felt. For despite the fact that man can reach for righteousness, he cannot perform it. He can aim for love, but he falls short. This is the heartbreaking experience of 20th-century man. "There is a passion and drive for cruel deeds which only the awe and fear of God can soothe; there is a suffocating selfishness in man which only holiness can ventilate." [6] The place where God and man meet is not at the place where man's powers give out but at the center, at the place where God calls man to love.

Do we need God? The question reveals that we no longer see clearly, for it is not God who is a problem but we. We may not need Him to "explain" our universe. (That should never have been the case.) Nor do we relate to Him only to secure our life. But as long as we seek to be men, we will need God to supply us with the power to love. And this He freely gives!

2
THINKING
ABOUT FAITH

In *The Seventh Seal,* a film set in 13th-century Sweden, Ingmar Bergman shows us a Knight just returned from a crusade who becomes locked in a grim duel with Death. Death meets the Knight once a day to carry on a game of chess. If he wins, he saves himself and his friends from falling into Death's power. If he is checkmated, Death takes them all.

The desperate contest is only the reflection of an even more arduous ordeal. Face to face with Death the Knight agonizes over questions of faith. He wants some sign, some assurance, that his faith in God is not in vain. "Is it so cruelly inconceivable," he cries out at one point, "to grasp God with the senses? Why would he hide himself in a mist of half-spoken promises and unseen miracles? I want knowledge, not faith, not supposition, but knowledge. I want God to stretch out his hand toward me, reveal himself, and speak to me." [1] His cry is not answered.

The Secret Question

The popularity of *The Seventh Seal* might be traced to the fact that Bergman's Knight utters the secret question of many hearts: Why must religion operate with faith in things unseen? Is faith possible for a person living in a scientific age? Could we not dispense with faith and relate to God in some other way? What is this thing called faith? Few people avoid asking themselves these questions, and those who take religion seriously are deeply involved in them. Faith has always been a daring adventure of the human spirit, but in our day there seems to be a deeper awareness of just how bold an enterprise it really is. To change the metaphor, we live at a time when the winds are fierce that blow at faith's candle. If we are to keep the candle lit, we need among other things to think clearly about what it means to believe.

It is surprising that so few Christians have paused to think about faith itself. Faith is so central to the religious life that it is taken for granted. Religion *is* faith for most people. (In popular speech we refer to a man's faith as meaning his religion.) It hardly seems possible to analyze faith without having religion itself dissolve before our eyes. Nevertheless there are at least two distinct ways in which *faith* is used both in popular speech and in the Bible. If we separate the two meanings, we will have taken a long step toward understanding what it means to have faith.

Faith and Knowledge

In common usage faith is first of all a way of knowing in religion. If someone asks us, "How do you know that what your religion says is true?" we ordinarily reply with the word *faith*. The Book of Hebrews gives us the classical description of faith in this sense: "Now faith is the assurance of things hoped for, the conviction of things not seen." God and the world of the spirit, obviously, are among the things not seen. Yet for the Christian they are realities, not illusions. The description of faith in Hebrews is accurate: faith is first the perception of unseen reality.

This understanding of faith challenges the prevailing notion that there is but one way to know "what is out there." For many people who operate by common sense the only way

25

we really know anything is by seeing. As Tennyson said:

> We have but faith; we cannot know,
> For knowledge is of things we see.

On a more sophisticated level this is known as the empirical or scientific approach to reality. The scientific method assumes that to know something we must be able to measure it in some way. Even if we cannot see the object of our investigation with our eyes, scientific instruments must be able to record data that will enable us to recognize that it is there. Turning the scientific method around, many people believe that whatever cannot be measured cannot be known. The "feeling for fact" is the hard-nosed attitude by which many moderns approach reality. Beliefs must be built only on the basis of measurable fact and on nothing else. Bertrand Russell once said the rational man is one who always proportions the degree of intensity with which he holds his various beliefs to the amount of evidence available for each.

Critical Faith

The Christian who operates with faith may agree that seeing is believing, but he adds that there are some things he can believe without seeing. In other words, the Christian holds that there is the possibility of a different kind of knowledge, one that does not rest solely on empirical investigation or personal sense experience. At this point we all become cautious. If we open the door to believing things that are not seen, if we accept them as realities, there appears to be no defense against the wildest superstitions or the most abysmal credulity. People at one time believed in witches, ghosts, goblins, and other creatures of fantasy. If they had believed only in the things they actually saw, they would have saved themselves much unhappiness. Their faith — their believing things they did not see — led them astray.

Christians are convinced that the way of faith does not open the door to such evil imaginations. Faith does not dispense with reason or with the critical view of the world by which such imaginations can be counteracted. Faith is no wild leap into the darkness of fantasy. It does not desire to live by myths or fairy stories any more than would any other serious human activity. Fairy stories may be charming, but they are not the stuff of faith. Faith always seeks to stay in touch with facts, with reality. Myth is the enemy of faith. We are not just pretending when we believe. That is why there should be no talk of "blind faith" in Christian experience. There is a sense in which faith remains open to revision, but it does not concede its grasp of unseen reality.

A Mistaken View

Some Christians, however, may misunderstand how faith functions. They value faith in proportion to its difficulty. In their view, the harder it is to believe something, the better the faith that believes it. Thus if a word from God came asking us to deny the fact that we saw a mountain before our very eyes, "great" faith would say that the mountain was not there. This is an example of the confusion that surrounds the subject of faith. Genuine faith does not contradict what we surely know to be true. Faith ends up as daring trust in God, as we shall see, but that trust is never abused. God does not force us to deny the reality of things we know in fact exist, or to accept the reality of things we know in fact do not exist. If to be a believer one had to suppress what he empirically knew to be true, no intelligent person could be a believer. This is not what is meant by the "absurdity" of faith, despite what some Christians think.

The Basis for Faith

If faith is no exercise in imagination, on what is it based? Where does faith as the conviction of things unseen come from? The answer consists of a number of things in combination. First, the believer becomes aware of unseen reality through his observation of the world about him. "The heavens declare the glory of God," said the psalmist. The universe is not present to the believer merely as a matter of fact. Rather, it is a source of awe and wonder that points to a reality beyond itself.[2] The believer is struck by the mystery of existence and senses the presence of Another in that mystery. But the form of the Other would remain vague and indistinct were it not for the second source of Christian faith, the Bible. The Bible is the record of God's self-disclosure in history, which reinforces and substantiates His revelation in nature. The Christian's reading of both nature and history combines to produce a personal conviction of God's realness and activity in the world. Thus faith is not generated by imagination but springs up in response to something outside the believer.

In drawing his conclusions the believer is not without certain assumptions. He confesses to a desire to believe, to a "will to believe," as William James called it. This in no way prejudices the believer's convictions. It means simply that *truth does not come to those who do not wish to find it.* In any field of investigation the observer has to enter in on what he is looking for to grasp it.[3] He cannot arbitrarily impose his own meanings on the facts, but at the same time he knows that the facts do not leap up and beat him into understanding what their significance might be. A scientist looking through a microscope has to want to make sense out of what he sees, otherwise the facts will mean nothing. Similarly a person has to want to find order, meaning, and the character of the mysterious Other who is contained in the universe about him if he is to become a believer.

Faith is a "believing seeing," someone has said, an interpretation of the facts in such a way as to reveal what they say of unseen reality. The "bias" of the believer in favor of finding something or Someone "out there" is really the logical presupposition for faith. Some kind of personal commitment has to be made before we can see things truthfully. This is why the skeptic, as skeptic, cannot become a believer. He withholds the very thing that makes faith possible: the desire to believe.

Before proceeding any further, let me point out something about the argument so far. I have *not* claimed that the reality of God can be proved to the satisfaction of someone who operates solely with an empirical approach to reality. That is impossible, for reasons I have just stated. What I have claimed, however, is that faith involves a reasonable activity of the human mind, and that is important. People are sometimes led to believe that to have faith a person must take leave of his senses, as if faith were something outlandish or at least odd. Faith is a daring adventure of the human spirit, but it remains a reasonable one. It is an enterprise of normal people, not dervishes or madmen. If faith were possible only for a dervish, few people would become believers. Because it is not so, faith is a possibility for all of us.

The Skeptic

To return to the skeptic, I have long felt that his position was a curious one. Frequently I ask, "What would you want in the way of proof for the reality of God?" Many times the answer is like that given by Bertrand Russell some years ago. When he was asked what he would accept as evidence for God's realness, Russell replied, "A voice from the sky or a prediction of some future event." As brilliant a philosopher as Professor Russell certainly is, he did not mention how he would recognize the voice as coming from God and distinguish it from other natural phenomena.[4] Furthermore, Russell did not bother to examine the contradiction that would be implied if God, the Source of all that exists, were to manifest Himself physically within the creation He has made. Even sophomores in high school come to see the absurdity such manifestation involves. When people continue to ask for empirical evidence for God's reality, it only indicates that skepticism finally is a matter of the will, a choice the person has made, rather than a strictly logical conclusion to which the evidence leads.

But there is enough of the skeptic in all of

us to make us sympathize with him. Faith may be a reasonable activity of the human mind, but many days of the week it is not very satisfying. Instead of taking things on faith, we would much rather see and know them in the ordinary way. True, there are some who do not feel this way. Most of us, however, identify with the Knight in *The Seventh Seal.* John Updike has described the longing for visible and tangible reassurance more tenderly in his short story "Pigeon Feathers." A young lad encounters doubt for the first time in his life. One night while in bed he decides to try something:

> Though the experiment frightened him, he lifted his hands high into the darkness above his face and begged Christ to touch them. Not hard or long: the faintest, quickest grip would be final for a lifetime. His hands waited in the air, itself a substance, which seemed to move through his fingers; or was it the pressure of his pulse. He returned his hands beneath the covers uncertain if they had been touched or not. For would not Christ's touch be infinitely gentle? [5]

We may understand that faith is the conviction of things unseen, but the longing to see remains.

Faith and Sight

Surprisingly, it is the Bible that recognizes our concerns and identifies with our impatience. There is a frequent contrast in the Bible between seeing and believing. St. Paul tells his readers that in our earthly existence "we walk by faith, not by sight." He says to the Romans: "Now hope [here equivalent to faith] that is seen is not hope. For who hopes for what he sees?" We can

31

infer from this that the earliest believers had the same problems we have. The best known of the early Christians who preferred sight to faith, of course, was the apostle Thomas. The preservation of the account of Christ's appearance to Thomas is additional proof that first-century believers needed bolstering in the exercise of faith. The Biblical writers encourage their readers rather than chide them (1 Peter 1). It is remarkable how gently the Bible deals with the believer's desire to see.

But in addition to sympathizing with the believer's preference for sight over faith, the Bible holds out the hope that some day things will be different. "Now," says St. Paul, "we see in a mirror dimly, but then face to face. Now I know in part; then I shall understand fully, even as I have been fully understood" (1 Cor. 13:12 RSV). The believer looks forward to a time when the painful necessity for following God by faith will have passed away. Many people fail to recognize this as one of the really great promises of the Gospel. They either assume there is nothing more to come or else, like some of our most sensitive artists and film makers, sink into despair over the apparent hiddenness and silence of God. Real faith is aware of the fact that it would be better to see than to believe, but this does not prevent it from stretching forward and grasping those things that are not seen.

Why Faith?

But why should faith be required at all? Is God playing a game of blindman's buff with us? Is there a further explanation that would help us understand and accept our situation? The answer to these questions is located in the Biblical narrative of the fall of man into sin. According to Genesis man is a creature who is now estranged from God. Direct, immediate communion with God has not only ceased but would be dangerous. The Hebrews were always afraid that they might "see" God. If that were to happen, they felt they would die, for no sinner can look on the face of the Holy One and live. This conviction reveals a profound insight into the connection between God's invisibility and man's moral condition. *God's hiddenness expresses the contrast between the holy God and sinful man.* The hiddenness of God is part of the mystery of evil and is an inescapable feature of the human situation. The God of the Bible resists any attempt to force Him out of His hiddenness. But at the same time He does make Himself available to man. This is the ever-recurring wonder of revelation.

The greatest illustration of man's yearning to see God and of God's response is in chapter 33 of the Book of Exodus. After the mighty events of the Exodus and Mount Sinai, Moses, like Ingmar Bergman's Knight, still prays that God show him His glory. The Lord refuses the request. Even the one with whom the Lord speaks "as a man speaks to his friend" is not permitted to look on His face. But the Lord does not abandon Moses. He grants Moses a vision of His goodness. In a scene of tremendous dramatic power, the Lord says to Moses: "Behold, there is a place by Me where you shall stand upon the rock; and while My glory passes by I will put you in a cleft of the rock, and I will cover you with My hand until I have passed by; then I will take away My hand, and you shall see My back; but My face shall not be seen" (vv. 21-23 RSV). God's presence is revealed not in spectacle or signs or wonders, but in a vision of His goodness. This and this alone is what Moses "sees."

God's confrontation with Moses in Exodus makes plain the greatness of His revelation in Jesus Christ. When God reveals Himself in Christ, it is not as though He were popping out from behind a puppet show to give the audience a look at the man who really pulls the strings. God's revelation in Christ comes by way of what Christians call "incarnation" rather than demonstration. Christ is the supreme revelation of God because He is the supreme embodiment of God's goodness toward man. It is in Christ that man really understands the love God has for him. God does not play blindman's buff with man! But though His revelation in Christ is clear, God's presence remains hidden from the prying eyes of man. For the Christian this can be endured, since he knows God now as love; he has "seen" God's glory (love) in Christ, and that is sufficient for him. (Cf. John 14)

"I want knowledge, not faith, not supposition, but knowledge. I want God to stretch out his hand toward me, reveal himself, and speak to me." This yearning God has fulfilled, not in the way we might want or expect at first but in a way perfectly in harmony with His being and character and the conditions that now exist between God and man. He reveals himself even while remaining hidden from us, and calls on us to exercise faith in its second sense: faith as trust.

The Real Adventure

Trust also involves an element of the unseen. If you give me your word that you will meet me somewhere at a certain time or if you declare to me that you want to be my friend, I must trust you and take you at your word. No visible assurance is possible in either instance. This is the kind of situation in which the believer finds himself. He understands that God is for him in Jesus Christ. On the basis of that Word from God, he entrusts himself into God's hands. With this the believer reaches the highest rung of faith and is in line for the compliment paid by Christ to those "who have not seen and yet believed." It is when faith as a grasp of unseen reality evolves into daring trust in the goodness and mercy of God that the real adventure of faith begins.

After the return of cosmonaut Ghermann Titov from his space flight, Premier Khrushchev of the Soviet Union is reported to have said that the cosmonaut had seen no sign of God in outer space. According to the Russian radio the flight dealt a "crushing blow to the idea of the existence of God." The blow is crushing only to those who persist in the notion that seeing is the sole way to believing. The Christian believer has perceived more of reality than the cosmonaut. He has viewed nature and history and God's self-disclosure that they contain. From that has come "the victory that overcomes the world, our faith." (1 John 5:4 RSV)

3
THE AGONY
OF DOUBT

A. LEONARD GRIFFITH, preacher at the City Temple, London, recounts the H. G. Wells story about the worried archbishop. Ordinarily the archbishop was one who dispensed advice and encouragement to others, but now he was in need. As he thought about his problems, it occurred to him to do what he had so often advised others to do. He would try prayer. Of course he had been saying his prayers regularly for years but never for anything that really involved his personal needs. The archbishop always regarded prayer as a beneficial exercise, like brushing teeth. He thought of prayer only dimly as a conversation with One who was really listening "out there," but that did not deter him. Yes, he would pray.

The archbishop retired to his own private chapel. There he sank to his knees, folded his hands, and began, "O God . . ." Then he paused. A voice, distinct and strong, neither friendly nor hostile, said, "Yes, what is it?" In the morning they found the archbishop's body. He had slipped off the step on which he had been kneeling and lay sprawled out on the red carpet of the chapel. It was obvious his death had been instantaneous.

Certainty Eroded

H. G. Wells intended his story as a satire, and most readers agree that it effectively homes in on its target. But in mocking religious pretension Wells at the same time exposes something that lies close to the surface of modern life. The case of the unfortunate archbishop is evidence for the radical skepticism that challenges religious belief in our day. In previous centuries bishops as pillars of the church could be counted on to hold the faith firmly, but in the 20th century, Wells seems to be saying, even bishops doubt. Recent years have produced some unexpected confirmations of Wells's contention as prominent churchmen make headlines with their misgivings about certain important Christian teachings.

What puts the doubts of bishops in the man-bites-dog category is the fact that Christian faith traditionally implies certainty and conviction. The model Christian is the one who is confident in his faith. "I am sure . . ." is the way St. Paul begins his ringing conclusion to chapter 8 of Romans. "Here I stand," proclaimed Luther with courage evidently bred of certainty. Christians have traditionally viewed doubt as the direct opposite of faith. No real Christian should succumb to the kind of self-deception displayed by the archbishop. The edifice of faith cannot stand on the shifting sands of doubt.

Some Christians would go further. They see doubt not only as evidence of a sick faith but as blasphemy. For if God has spoken clearly and unmistakably, then to doubt is to commit the sin of pride. It was the Tempter who in the Garden of Eden first suggested, "Did God say . . . ?" When therefore the Christian begins to harbor doubts, he has succumbed to the Enemy and turned against God. Just as doubt corrodes relationships between persons, so it destroys a man's relationship to God. Christian faith ought to be an unqualified yes to everything God has said.

Unfortunately what ought to be and what is are two distinctly different matters. Christians have long recognized that doubt accompanies faith like a shadow. In our modern era, however, doubt regarding the truth of the faith seems, like a river at flood stage, to have overrun its banks and threatens to sweep everything away. This danger exists because not only are more Christians questioning their faith, but the questions they ask and the doubts they entertain are more radical than those of previous ages. Another time could be called "The Age of Faith." Ours has to be known as "The Age of Uncertainty."

Doubt Defended

From all that I have said about the danger of doubt, you would think that Christian writers would be busy warning people against it. Surprisingly, it is now the fashion to defend and encourage doubt. This has happened for two reasons. First, we have come to see that, sadly, many who profess to believe all that their faith teaches do so only out of ignorance or credulity. That kind of "believer" does not compare favorably with the person who gives Christianity careful consideration but believes he must reject it to be intellectually honest. Tennyson observed:

> There lives more faith in honest doubt,
> Believe me, than in half the creeds.

Second, as M. Holmes Hartshorne has said, "we cannot exist as human beings without thinking—and to think is to question, to probe, to criticize." [1] Doubt is a necessary part of a person's growth. Without it he cannot fully appropriate what he experiences. To interdict doubt is to condemn a man to perpetual intellectual childhood. As a matter of fact, it is impossible for a mature individual to take everything solely on authority. He has the right and the duty for the sake of personal integrity to ask questions before committing himself.

In acknowledging the role of doubt we must not, however, overlook an important distinction. It is one thing to ask questions about the faith; it is quite another to call the faith into question. *The difference does not lie in the questions asked but in the heart of the questioner.* A believer can ask questions to enlarge his understanding of the faith without affecting his basic commitment. The doubter puts his questions precisely because he is insecure in his commitment. While doubt, like other painful experiences, can have positive effects, it would be foolish to encourage it for that reason. That would be like telling a person to contract a disease because some people grow in fortitude and charity under suffering. To encourage questions about the faith, especially from young people, is all to the good, for the failure to confront the hard questions at an early age can have disastrous results. But nothing is gained by telling someone to doubt.

The more one thinks about it, encouraging doubt is really a carrying-coals-to-Newcastle type of activity. It is the rare Christian who escapes doubt in some form. That there *are* such Spirit-filled believers I will not deny, but their numbers seem to be far smaller than those of occasional or chronic doubters. Most of us (even church school children!) do a lot of wondering about the faith. Our inner ears have all heard the seductive song of Sportin' Life in *Porgy and Bess:*

> It ain't necessarily so,
> It ain't necessarily so.
> De t'ings dat yo' li'ble
> To read in de Bible—
> It ain't necessarily so.[2]

Doubt Avoided

Doubt is a painful and distressing experience that no one likes to face. To avoid it Christians frequently resort to various stratagems. Some say, "I don't pretend to understand all these mysteries. I'll just believe what the church tells me to believe." This is the way of fideism or "blind" faith, the exercise of faith without thought or reflection. For Protestant Christians fideism is impossible. Protestantism has always emphasized the necessity for personal, reasoned faith, since Luther declared at Worms that he would not recant unless convicted by Scripture and *plain reason.* Fideism appears to be virtuous, but it verges on and frequently becomes credulity.

A more popular way to avoid the problem of doubt is to hold that the question of factuality in religious matters isn't important. According to this view it doesn't matter whether the things Christianity has traditionally held are really so; what matters is only what these statements symbolize. Thus, in this view it is not important whether Jesus of Nazareth actually was raised from the dead. If we believe in man's survival in some manner beyond the grave, that is enough. We have grasped the reality of the Resurrection. In this view few doubts arise, because there is so little to doubt.

It is necessary to learn to think for oneself in matters of faith and become personally convinced of one's creed if faith is to be authentic. But an overemphasis on the subjective or existential aspect of faith can lead to the dissolution of the Christian religion. While all religious statements must be personally meaningful, this does not mean that it is immaterial whether faith includes *anything* beyond meaning for the individual. "If Christ has not been raised," St. Paul argues passionately, "your faith is in vain and you are most miserable." The apostle did not say that it would be all right to let the fact of Christ's resurrection disappear and only the meaning remain. He contended this would be a disaster, for faith has to do with truth, with the difference between reality and appearance.

Finally, there are those who go still further and argue that religion is never to be analyzed or made the subject of reflection. Faith is an experience, a matter of the heart, they say, and "the heart has its reasons that reason cannot know." This latter point is frequently made with a great deal of emphasis, and certainly it is a point well taken. Christians must recognize that intellectualism is a danger. But equating religion with feeling means the destruction of any objective basis for faith. Experience without reflection is sentimentalism, and that is too high a price to pay to get rid of doubt.

Doubt Confronted

Doubts must be faced, and the best way to face them is head on. To be a Christian means to follow truth wherever it leads, even at the risk of passing through the valley of the shadow of doubt. Often the person struggling for faith feels lonely and abandoned. At such times it is absolutely essential to recall that God is greater than our doubts even as He is greater than our sins, that He accepts us in the midst of our doubts and confusion (1 John 3:19-22). C. S. Lewis said that a believer is never closer to God than at the moment he feels abandoned and is left asking the question "Why?" Such might be said of the doubter. He can bring his doubts into the open because of the love of God. Christians often fail to meet doubt openly. (One faculty member told me that he feared to ask his questions because there might not be any answers, and that would embarrass the minister.) When doubt is covered up, however, it eats at faith from the inside until nothing is left but empty symbols and hollow rites. This need not happen.

Secure in the grace and mercy of God, the Christian in doubt can learn to employ the technique of keeping certain things in abeyance. The believer does not despair each time he encounters some difficulty in faith. If he cannot answer his questions immediately, the Christian can "put them on ice," leaving them until more information or study is available. This is different from ignoring or evading questions in matters of faith. It means that the Christian holds his questions in tension with faith and still functions as a Christian: attending church, saying prayers, receiving the Sacrament, serving the neighbor, using his resources for the cause of God in this world. Much of Christianity is this kind of "believing unbelief," as typified by the concerned father who said to Christ: "I believe; help my unbelief." No one will argue that this should be a permanent state of affairs, but it is good to know that a person can use this technique to pass to a higher level of conviction and confidence.

Faith in God, therefore, is possible even while certain questions are under review, not excepting the question of God Himself! The believer can attack his uncertainties free from guilt and confident of success. In his moments of uncertainty he has a right to expect the best from his fellow Christians in the church. The Christian with questions should be welcomed no matter how distressing his questions may be. Unfortunately, it must be admitted that some Christians, including the clergy, treat the seeker much like the barker at a carnival: "Go away, kid, you bother me." Usually this is an admission that the doubter has touched some hidden nerve and may be dealing with someone like H. G. Wells's archbishop. But while there are some like that archbishop around, there are, happily, far more Christians who are able and ready to help the honest doubter. The Christian in the struggle for faith is surrounded by a great cloud of witnesses, past and present, who can be of genuine assistance.

With such resources available, the doubter should not quit too easily. I have heard students declare, "I can't accept the Virgin Birth any longer." Usually they refer to it as the "Immaculate Conception," a totally different subject. Such assertions are really foolish and arrogant, no matter how sincere. Foolish, since the person often does not know what he is casting aside and has not given the matter the kind of consideration that would justify a rejection.[3] Arrogant, since he assumes that no one can possibly say anything that might be of service in meeting the difficulty. Even the sincere seeker may display a tendency to give up the faith as soon as his first attempts at arriving at clarity on a particular issue do not satisfy. A profound faith never issues from a relaxed attitude toward truth. Here again "we must through much tribulation enter into the kingdom of God." You can produce an acceptable meal from a TV dinner, you can learn to play the recorder in a half dozen easy lessons, but no one has as yet so packaged or simplified Christianity as to eliminate the necessity for sincere and diligent personal application on the part of those who seek faith.

Doubt Direct

To meet doubts successfully, it is well to recall that there are different kinds of challenges to Christian faith. The first is made up of direct assaults on the content of Christian faith. Sportin' Life's song is an example; his aim is to shake the confidence of his listeners in the "things that yo' li'ble /to read in the Bible." Had Sportin' Life been dealing with more sophisticated and better educated people than the simple citizens of Catfish Row, he would have questioned more important things than Jonah's being swallowed by a "whale" or David's killing Goliath with a slingshot. He might have raised doubts about key presuppositions held by the Biblical writers, such as the reality of God, revelation, the necessity of forgiveness. But that would have made a terrible song.

Far from flinching from an honest confrontation with this kind of doubt, the Christian faith welcomes it. Theologians have for a long time discussed the kind of questions Sportin' Life raised and have produced a vast amount of wise and helpful writing on each of these subjects. Many objections to Christian belief, even in an age of science, turn out to be versions of older questions of the past. Opponents of Christianity do not realize how often their "devastating" attacks are only variations on themes by more original heretics of the past.

As an example, consider this passage from the Greek writer Xenophanes of the fifth century B. C.:

> But mortals consider that the gods are born, and that they have clothes and speech and bodies like their own. The Ethiopians say that their gods are snub-nosed and black, the Thracians that theirs have light blue eyes and red hair. But if cattle and horses or lions had hands, or were able to draw with their hands and do the work that men can do, horses would draw the forms of the gods like horses, and cattle like cattle, and they would make their bodies such as they each had themselves.[4]

To the person who is thinking of it for the first time, the psychological objection against religion is shattering, for it appears to be something distinctly modern. As it turns out, the argument is not new at all. And if the argument is not new, it can be assumed that someone has analyzed it and offered a reply. All that one has to do is to locate the spokesman and weigh the argument against the reply.

It is true, however, that our modern era has given some of the old questions novel form and produced some new ones. St. Paul and his congregations did not have pocket editions of Freud's *The Future of an Illusion* or books on linguistic analysis and on evolution to deal with. Nevertheless, when Christians use the resources they have, they will find that the Christian faith can hold its own against all comers. This fact is seldom stated so baldly today, but it is true. By "holding its own" I do not mean that faith can be proved with mathematical certainty, for then faith would no longer be faith. What I mean is that Christians can demonstrate that arguments commonly used against the faith are invalid and the facts adduced to demolish religion are often erroneous or misused. Roadblocks in the way of faith can be cleared away with a good deal of strenuous bulldozing.

Nihilism

There is a far more dangerous form of doubt than the kind we have discussed up to now. The particular virulence of modern skepticism appears when Christianity and its teachings suddenly seem to lose any real significance. In days gone by the faith was at least important enough to controvert, even ridicule. Every village had its atheist or freethinker, and books like *The Bible Unmasked* sold well. Now, despite the universal claims of Christianity, large segments of the population go on their way without giving the faith a passing glance. This is the typical attitude of modern, urban man.

Recall the incident from *The Stranger,* by Albert Camus. The central figure of the book, a French Algerian, is being tried for murder. While in prison, the chaplain asks to see him but is refused. The chaplain visits him despite the rebuff.

> "Why," he asked, "don't you let me come to see you?"
>
> I explained that I didn't believe in God.
>
> "Are you really so sure of that?"
>
> I said I saw no point in troubling my head about the matter, whether I believed or didn't was, to my mind, a question of so little importance.

Later on the chaplain visits the prisoner again.

> All of a sudden he swung around on me, and burst out passionately: "No! No! I refuse to believe it. I'm sure you often wished there was an afterlife." Of course I had, I told him. Everybody has that wish at times. But that had no more importance than wishing to be rich, or to swim fast, or to have a better-shaped mouth. . . . I went up close up to him and made a last attempt to explain that I'd very little time left, and I wasn't going to waste it on God.[5]

The Christian church is still struggling to adjust to this mood, a mood in which there are no questions because the whole subject is not considered worth the bother. The church's response to the world of antiheroes and nihilism has not been adequate.

Without going into the matter any further, I believe the chief value the figure of the Stranger serves is to make us examine our religious doubts more closely. How much does our faith mean to us? Does it really concern us ultimately, to the limit, or are we playing games? There is a stage when such questions can still be heard and the significance of the Christian faith still be seen. The individual who undertakes a reexamination of faith at that point will see that Christianity does have to do with things that matter, that there are beliefs worth dying for. Those who think like the Stranger often are making the mistake of divorcing God from life. They fail to see that to deny God is to deny life as well.

Religious Doubt

A final category of doubt is the most difficult of all. This is religious doubt in the strict sense of the word. The questions such doubters raise do not deal with the reality of the faith or its significance. The religious doubter leaves the entire structure of faith intact, but he agonizes over the question of his own place in that structure. He does not raise the question of God's existence but the question of divine grace. The struggle is not with nothingness but with the attitude of God. Like the father of the murdered girl in Ingmar Bergman's film *The Virgin Spring*, he cries out, "God, I do not understand You." He wonders why God seems to play hide-and-seek. For this person God is the enemy. His agony arises from the apparent absence or silence of a God who hides Himself.

The record of man's spiritual life reveals that there have been many who have passed through such a "dark night of the soul." Nowhere do we find a more moving description of the encounter with the silent-absent-enemy God than in the Book of Job. "Oh, that I knew where I might find Him, that I might come even to His seat!" cried Job. ". . . Behold, I go forward, but He is not there; and backward, but I cannot perceive Him" (Job 23:3, 8). Others who have come after Job have experienced something of the same. Some ages, it appears, experience particular forms of religious doubt more acutely than others. In the age of the Reformation men struggled with the question of predestination, as Martin Luther's letters of spiritual counsel indicate. Our age is obsessed with the silence and hiddenness of God, a doubt answered only by a new confrontation with Jesus Christ as God's reply to man's search for the hidden God.

As long as man is partitioned from realms

of glory, he will have to suffer the "whining gnats of doubt." We may devoutly wish that it weren't so, that faith would encounter no obstacles, but lamenting our condition is a sterile response to something that has to be faced boldly and creatively. While we now see only the reversed images of heavenly realities as in a mirror, to use the figure Paul taught us, there surely will come a time when we shall be able to turn around to enjoy the heavenly vision directly. Then all doubts will disappear. Like those who preceded us who

>Wrestled hard, as we do now,
>With sins, and doubts, and fears

we shall know even as we are known.

4
THE SILENCE
OF GOD

In 1963 a remarkable play, *The Deputy*, by Rolf Hochhuth, opened in Berlin. The work was not remarkable for its artistic merit (it was severely criticized for its lack of dramatic craftsmanship) nor for the acting, which was adequate but not great. The sensational feature of *The Deputy* was its indictment of Pope Pius XII for his alleged failure to speak out on behalf of the Jews during World War II. Wherever the play was produced, feelings ran so high that the police had to be on hand to prevent the outbreak of violence. In one German city members of the audience leaped from their seats and attempted a physical assault on the actors. Hochhuth's invention plainly had struck some raw nerves.

The furor which *The Deputy* raised obscured some important themes the author had woven into the play. The question of the Vatican's relations with Hitler finally matters more to Roman Catholics than anyone else, but the question of the silence of God, which Hochhuth introduces in the fifth act, involves us all. Ricardo Fontana, a young Jesuit, has voluntarily given himself into the hands of the Nazis to accompany the Jews whom, he believes, his church has failed. The camp doctor taunts him with the meaninglessness of his anonymous sacrifice. Ricardo replies:

> Do you think God would overlook a sacrifice, merely
> because the killing is done without pomp and circumstance?
> Your ideas can't be as primitive as that!

The doctor retorts:

> Aha, you think God does not overlook

the sacrifice! Really?

You know, at bottom, all my work's concerned
entirely with this one question. Really, now,
I'm doing all I can.

Since July of '42 for fifteen months,
weekdays and Sabbath, I've been sending people
to God.

Do you think he's made the slightest acknowl-
edgment?

He has not even directed a bolt of lightning against
me.

Can you understand that?

You ought to know.

Nine thousand in one day a while back.[1]

The Challenge of Evil

Hochhuth, of course, is but one writer among
many who have brooded over the problem of
God's apparent silence in the face of the suffering of the helpless and the innocent. The problem
is as old as the Scriptures. But Hochhuth saw
that the terrible events of World War II gave the
ancient question a new and horrifying intensity.
Never before had mankind experienced such
a gigantic escalation of cruelty, evil, and suffering. The ashes of Auschwitz, Belsen, Dachau,
Buchenwald, and Treblinka haunt the memory
of the race. No one can think of those melancholy
places or enter one of the solemn memorials
erected to the victims of the holocaust without
raising the question of God. Why? Where was
He? Does He exist?

I have said that being a believer isn't easy.
There are many sorts of difficulties for the believer to contend with in the struggle for faith:
philosophical problems, problems presented by

the Biblical narrative, the offensive life of supposed Christians. Many a person has been disil-
lusioned and driven to doubt by the church's
foot-dragging on social issues such as the Negro
drive for equality. But all these are so many
chess problems compared to the threat to faith
posed by the silence of God in the face of suffering. Faith can keep going under heavy fire. It
can surmount many obstacles, even severe personal suffering. But God's apparent silence when
the innocent suffer is a vital wound that often
proves fatal.

In Archibald MacLeish's modern drama, the
character J. B. was tormented by Nickles' chant:

If God is God He is not good,
If God is good He is not God.[2]

Nickles' couplet capsulizes man's shocked reaction to a God who seems to pay no attention to
man's suffering. In effect the little verse puts God
on trial. It demands an answer, although it is plain
that the speaker expects no successful defense.

God on Trial

The idea of putting God on trial strikes us
as blasphemous until we recall that the Bible's
portrayal of Job is of one who seeks God in order
to call Him to account. Job wants to know the
reason for his undeserved suffering. Richard
Luecke comments: "When Thomas Aquinas took
up the question of how Job could presume to
argue with God, he concluded that if truth or
justice are at issue, the status of the disputant
does not really matter." [3] The trial can proceed.

"If God is God He is not good." The twin
ideas of "Love almighty and ills unlimited"
(Austin Farrer) are too much for the human mind

to take. There is justification for some pain and suffering from a biological point of view. Were it not for pain, the body would not know when it is in danger of harming itself or of being harmed. We recognize that pain that descends on a person as the result of crime or moral wrong is in some sense deserved, hence comprehendable. We also perceive that a great deal of pain is inflicted by man in his inhumanity against his fellowman and cannot be viewed as God's "fault," although the problem begins to arise here. Much of the suffering brought about by the Nazi regime or by patterns of segregation in America has to be laid at the doorsteps of those who allowed such evils to arise: good men who did nothing.

But the pain that wrings our hearts is that which serves no biological function, which is not deserved, which whether inflicted by the wickedness of men or by accident (an "act of God"!) falls on the uncomprehending and the defenseless. How can God "permit" a virus to deform a child as yet unborn? How is it possible that He who rules the wind and waves withholds the rain that feeds the hungry people of India? How does He allow a Nazi guard to dash a child to death for the sake of an apple? The bewilderment of the human being in the face of these questions is reflected in the sorrowful musing of the central figure in John Updike's novel *Rabbit, Run.* In a drunken stupor brought on by Rabbit's infidelity to her, the wife accidentally permits the baby to drown in its bath.

> He goes into the bathroom and the water is still in the tub. Some of it has seeped away so the top of the water is an inch below a faint gray line on the porcelain but the tub is still more than half

full. A heavy, calm volume, odorless, tasteless, colorless, the water shocks him like the presence of a silent person in the bathroom. Stillness makes a dead skin on its unstirred surface. There's even a kind of dust on it. He rolls back his sleeve and reaches down and pulls the plug; the water swings and the drain gasps. He watches the line of water slide slowly and evenly down the wall of the tub, and then with a crazed vortical cry the last of it is sucked down. He thinks how easy it was, yet in all His strength God did nothing. Just that little rubber stopper to lift.[4]

It is apparent that men have difficulty imagining a God who allows the weak and the innocent to suffer in silence. Only a monster would do that, and there have been some who have not hesitated to depict God in that way. After waiting expectantly for God to appear to her, the insane girl in another Bergman film, *Through a Glass, Darkly,* is driven to hysteria by what she finally does see. In her mind God appears not as One who brings peace and light but as a spider. The "spider-God" motif recurs in a number of Bergman films. For Bergman, deeply sensitive to the world's suffering, it is the only kind of God conceivable. The film maker says what many have only thought.

"If God is good He is not God." The only way for God to be exonerated of the charge of cruelty, so it seems, is to hold that He is the victim of a force that at times is superior to Him. In that case we could believe that God does not really intend for His creatures to suffer. He might mean them to be happy and exempt from evil, but sometimes the opposition gets the better of the battle. For a long time in the history of Christianity (and even earlier) *dualism,* as the idea of two opposing gods or divine forces is called, was a widely held point of view that enabled people to make some sense out of the presence of evil. Even today some theologians argue that a kind of a limited dualism has to be assumed if we are to do justice to the facts. The point is valid, but in the final analysis the problem remains.

If we seriously mean to say that there is a force or power that is superior to God even for a moment, God then ceases to be God. His exoneration would be purchased at the price of His Godhead, for by definition God must be that to which nothing is superior. The recognition of a force greater than God would mean God's dethronement and the elevation of a new god. A God who occasionally goes down before the forces of evil would merit only man's sympathy, not his worship or adoration. Isaiah taunts the idol worshipers because they have to take care of a god who cannot take care of himself. Believers in a God who is second best would find themselves subject to the same ridicule.

God Defended

As they pondered the dilemma posed by God's omnipotence and the experience of suffering, Christians of the past have attempted to "justify the ways of God to man," to develop *theodicies,* as such lines of reasoning were called. What they produced turned out at times to be dangerously superficial. For example, William Cowper's

> Judge not the Lord by feeble sense,
> But trust Him for His grace;
> Behind a frowning providence
> He hides a smiling face

must seem frivolous to survivors of an earthquake or a saturation bombing. Before they learned better, spokesmen for the Christian belief in the goodness of God despite suffering and evil were often easy targets for sharpshooting critics. Voltaire's poem written after the disastrous November 1, 1755, earthquake at Lisbon, Portugal, and his satirical novel *Candide* closed the door once and for all on any simplistic resolution of the problem of evil. If any approach to the question is to be found, it cannot refuse to measure the full tragedy of the human condition.

God Rejected

In real life millions no longer consider Nickles' couplet a problem. They have escaped the dilemma of a God who is cruel or a God who is weak simply by saying that there is no God at all. For many people it is far more tolerable to believe that no God exists than to accept the coexistence of both God and suffering. If mankind must suffer, at least it should not have to do so wondering why God does not speak or help. A certain kind of admirable, if desperate, courage can be noted in some who believe that mankind faces alone "the trampling march of unconscious power." Despairing of the possibility for discovering meaning in the human experience, atheistic existentialism turns to face the absurdity of life with resolution and compassion. Albert Camus was one like this. In our time he has come to be regarded a nonreligious saint.

At first sight atheism appears to be the strong man's answer to the problem of evil. Here is man, like Captain Ahab in Melville's *Moby Dick*, shaking his fist in the face of the cosmos, declaring his independence of any need for God, and bravely facing his destiny alone. But on second thought, such an atheism turns out to be more emotional reaction than a conclusion demanded by strict logic. Countervailing the power of God against the obvious fact of evil in the universe, Nickles' intention was to abolish the notion of God entirely. A God who is not good is inconceivable to him and to those who choose atheism because of evil. But for the religionist the problem is located precisely in the possibility that God may *not* be good. The religionist does not permit evil to obliterate God: evil simply makes the question of God more acute than ever. That is why the believer is the really tough-minded man. He is contending with the problem of innocent suffering on a profounder level than the atheist. Nothing in the fact of evil says God does not exist. *That* is the frightening prospect Job wrestles with:

> Behold, I go forward, but He is not there; and backward, but I cannot perceive Him; on the left hand I seek Him, but I cannot behold Him; I turn to the right hand, but I cannot see Him. . . . Therefore I am terrified at His presence; when I consider, I am in dread of Him. God has made my heart faint; the Almighty has terrified me; for I am hemmed in by darkness, and thick darkness covers my face. (Job 23:8, 15-17 RSV)

The Verdict

Martin Luther once said that God governs the external affairs of the world in such a way that if you regard them and follow what you see, you are forced to conclude either that there is no God or that God is unjust. If the first conclusion is to be rejected as a refusal to face up to the fact of evil, what of the second? Is God unjust? What happens when God is tried for the suffering of the innocent, the pain and evil in His world? One answer is given in *The Sign of Jonah,* a play by Guenter Rutenborn produced in Germany shortly after World War II. The drama deals with the terrible memories of the recent war. Characters switch back and forth from their real identities in life to their stage roles, seeking to discover the one who is guilty for what had happened. The conclusion gradually dawns on them that God is the guilty one. Average Woman cries out at last:

> God is guilty! That's true! True! True! . . . I ask, where was the God we were taught to call Father? He has failed just as this Court must fail,
> because the children aren't here to accuse Him with their emaciated, decayed bodies, and with eyes hollow from hunger and terror. . . .

The Judge asks for the verdict. Average Man and Average Woman pass sentence:

> God shall become a human being, a wanderer on earth,
> deprived of His rights, homeless, hungry, thirsty, in constant fear of death.
> He shall be born to a woman, somewhere along a country road, and the moans of the poor creature shall
> ring in His ears day and night.
> He shall be surrounded by the feeble, the sick, the filthy, by people bearing the marks of leprosy.
> Rotting corpses shall bar His path.
> He shall know what it means to die.
> He, Himself, shall die! And lose a son,
> and suffer the agonies of fatherhood.

To which the Queen adds:

> And when at last He dies, He shall be disgraced
> and ridiculed.

Three Archangels embellish the sentence:

> I, Gabriel, shall go to a country ruled by cruel,
> parasitic men, a divided land occupied by a for-
> eign power.
>
> I shall go to a virgin named Mary.
>
> She shall bring God into the world, under sus-
> picion of
>
> shame — and as a Jew!

> I, Michael, shall order the Heavenly Hosts to let
> Him walk
>
> the earth unprotected. When He falls to His knees,
>
> when the curse of being a man sends sweat drip-
> ping
>
> from His brow like drops of blood, I shall grant
> Him
>
> sufficient strength only that He may go on suffering,
>
> shall console Him as He consoled the faithful,
>
> putting them off with promises so that they can
> bear
>
> more suffering.

> I, Raphael, shall be present when He sinks into
> death,
>
> and I shall stand by His grave and be the horror's
> holiest witness that God is dead! [5]

In Rutenborn's drama, the final touch is provided when the Judge who passes the verdict
is revealed to be God Himself.

The Suffering God

What *The Sign of Jonah* gives us is religious
truth with authentic redemptive power. The

mystery of innocent suffering is enveloped and neutralized by an even greater mystery, the mystery of a God who identifies and suffers with His creatures. Innocent suffering appears absurd, but not when God, the Ground of being, is somehow in that suffering. For then God turns out to be not one who sits high above the battle, callously urging man to keep a stiff upper lip, nor one who cruelly sports with man as a cat does with its prey. God is seen as the One who stands beside the sufferer and shares his pain. God endures precisely what man would have Him endure were he to put God on trial!

God's participation in human pain is vastly more than an expression of sympathy. Here truth outruns drama. In Jesus Christ God overcomes suffering through suffering; He destroys evil by being made evil's victim. The crucifixion of the Son of God ends in the triumph of the resurrection on the third day. But what God experiences in Jesus Christ, is not something endured only because of some "sentence" imposed on Him. It is rather love's offering to a tortured humanity for mankind's deliverance. The resurrection of the Crucified reveals that suffering is neither meaningless nor powerless. However terrible the ordeal may be, strength flows from the fact that the sufferer's experience is a participation in the sufferings of Jesus Christ (Colossians 1:24), who is ultimately the Victor.

Dietrich Bonhoeffer wrote at the end of his life: "The God who makes us live in the world without using him as a working hypothesis is the God before whom we are ever standing. . . . Matthew 8:17 makes it crystal clear that it is not by his omnipotence that Christ helps us, but by his weakness and suffering." [6] We may wonder why God chooses to deal with evil in this manner. We may shake our heads in amazement that God would clothe His power in weakness as He does in Jesus Christ, placing Himself entirely under the conditions of human life, subject to all life's evils. That is all right, for wonder and amazement are appropriate reactions to the mystery of God's self-imposed weakness, which is His power. The problem of evil ends with no philosophical "answer" but is taken up into a reality that is greater than itself: the suffering love of God. Men are not called to cerebration but to worship.

When we learn to approach the problem of suffering via the mystery of Jesus Christ, we have learned to distinguish between what Luther called God hidden and God revealed. The God whom we confront in nature and history outside of Jesus Christ is a God who is masked, a God who baffles and terrifies. But it is not this God with whom we have to do. The God who is God for us is God revealed in Jesus Christ. In Christ man sees God as He really is. In Christ God reveals that He is for man, not against him, and that His ways are the ways of love. It is wrong to say that God has left man to suffer in silence, that the "transmitter has gone dead" before bringing a healing word from outside. God speaks in Jesus Christ. It is when men refuse Christ as the Word that God is considered either cruel or nonexistent. Then the suffering of the innocent drives men to despair or to the brave but empty resolution of those who call life an absurdity, unable to account for even the good with which life is crammed.

Thinkers and artists and ordinary men down

through the ages have pondered the mystery of evil, sometimes in resignation, often in anger at the God whom they hold responsible. It is not often that artists illumine man's suffering with the Crucified. Helen Waddell's story *Peter Abelard* is one such attempt. The problem of animal pain is a subject that we could not consider in the space of this chapter. Our concern was human suffering, the suffering of the innocent. But what Thibault tells Abelard has much to do with our topic. The scene is one in which the two men hear the cry of a rabbit suddenly caught in a trap. They run to release it, but they are too late.

It lay for a moment breathing quickly, then in some blind recognition of the kindness that had met it at last, the small head thrust and nestled against his arm, and it died.

It was that last confiding thrust that broke Abelard's heart. He looked down at the little draggled body, his mouth shaking. "Thibault," he said, "do you think there is a God at all? Whatever has come to me, I earned it. But what did this one do?"

Thibault nodded.

"I know," he said. "Only—I think God is in it too."

Abelard looked up sharply.

"In it? Do you mean that it makes Him suffer, the way it does us?"

Again Thibault nodded.

"Then why doesn't He stop it?"

"I don't know," said Thibault. "Unless—unless it's like the Prodigal Son. I suppose the father could have kept him at home against his will. But what would have been the use? All this," he stroked the limp body, "is because of us. But all the time God suffers. More than we do."

Abelard looked at him, perplexed.

"Thibault, when did you think of all this?"

Thibault's face stiffened. "It was that night," he said, his voice strangled. "The things we did to—to poor Guibert. He—" Thibault stopped. "I could not sleep for nights and nights. And then I saw that God suffered too. And I thought I would like to be a priest."

"Thibault, do you mean Calvary?"

Thibault shook his head. "That was only a piece of it—the piece that we saw—in time. Like that." He pointed to a fallen tree beside them, sawn through the middle. "That dark ring there, it goes up and down the whole length of the tree. But you only see it where it is cut across. That is what Christ's life was; the bit of God that we saw. And we think God is like that, because Christ was like that, kind, and forgiving sins and healing people. We think God is like that for ever, because it happened once, with Christ. But not the pain. Not the agony at the last. We think that stopped."

Abelard looked at him, the blunt nose and the wide mouth, the honest troubled eyes. He could have knelt before him.

"Then Thibault," he said slowly, "you think that all this," he looked down at the little quiet body in his arms, "all the pain of the world, was Christ's cross?"

"God's cross," said Thibault. "And it goes on."

"The Patripassian heresy," muttered Abelard, mechanically. "But, oh God, if it were true. Thibault, it must be. At least there is something back of it that is true. And if we could find it—it would bring back the whole world." [7]

5
THE WAY
TO CHRIST

VOLTAIRE ONCE PAID A VISIT to a mountaintop early in the morning. Viewing the grandeur that the rising sun created, the great French philosopher and wit fell to his knees and cried, "God, I believe." Then as he rose and dusted himself off he added, "But regarding monsieur, the Son, and madame, his Mother, that is quite another matter."

What Voltaire said in jest forms the heart of many a person's problem with the Christian faith. There have always been people who express admiration for Christianity as a system of ethics, so much so that they would be content to equate the Christian faith with the Sermon on the Mount (as they read it) and a little God thrown in. The idea of a divine Christ is "quite another matter." But the majority of both Christians and non-Christians recognizes this interpretation of the historic faith as an oddity, no matter how often it is tried.

On entering the new Anglican cathedral in Coventry, England, the first thing to greet the visitor's eye is Sutherland's gigantic tapestry of "Christ in Glory," which hangs over the high altar. The same scene, this time done in ceramic tile as an 80-foot reredos, is the focal point of the Roman Catholic cathedral in Hartford, Conn. Protestants and Catholics alike confess the centrality and uniqueness of Jesus Christ. Christianity without a divine Christ, as the church came to understand early in its history, would be a contradiction in terms.

Christ and the Creeds

For the average person the problem with Christ's divinity first arises in connection with the historic creeds of the church. If one is to believe in Jesus Christ—and this is obviously necessary to be a Christian—one ought to be able to repeat the words of the creeds sincerely. Many people become aware of their difficulty with the Christian faith when they discover how hard it is for them to confess the Second Article of the Apostles' Creed in the Sunday service. I have known people who would conscientiously refrain from uttering the words that caused them uneasiness even as a matter of form, much to their credit. People are sensitive to issues of faith, especially to belief in a divine Christ. Again and again the creeds occasion the statement, "I believe in God, but I can't accept what the church says about Jesus." The words are spoken honestly, without belligerence or hostility. Implicit is often a request for help. In this chapter I propose a functional approach to the question of Christ's divinity as a way to overcome some of the barriers blocking an affirmation of Christ as Lord.

First, a word about the origin of the creeds, by which we mean particularly the Apostles' and the Nicene Creeds, both held in common by the large majority of Christians to this day. Most of the great Christian creeds and confessions were drawn up as the church's response to a particular challenge to the faith at a definite point in history. The Nicene Creed, for example, with its elaborate confession of faith in Christ, was composed about A. D. 325 in reply to the teachings of a certain Arius, who held that Jesus was to be detached from God and numbered among His creatures. Against Arius the church declared that Jesus is "God of God, Light of Light, Very God of Very God, begotten, not made, being of one substance with the Father, by whom all things were made." Such language is difficult for moderns. We do not think in terms of "substance" or "being." Our view of reality is dynamic rather than static. Some of the difficulty people have with the Christian faith is traceable to the distance between the creeds and the way we express ourselves today. When we question creedal language, it does not always mean that we have come into conflict with the Christian faith.

Christ and the Scriptures

To understand what the creeds mean when they speak about Christ we have to go back to the Scriptures as the original witness to Jesus Christ, since creeds are the church's reflection on the Biblical statement, "God was in Christ." The Bible's reports about Jesus are a curious blend of the familiar and the unfamiliar. On the one hand Jesus is born of His mother, Mary, in a town that exists to this day. He works at a trade known to us all and becomes a wandering preacher, an unusual but not wholly unimaginable occupation. His message is cast in strange modes of thought, but we understand it easily as a message asking for a radical righteousness and proclaiming an equally radical concept of the grace of God. Many of His sayings have become household words. His running conflict with the religious and secular authorities leads to His arrest and trial. Finally, He is executed on orders of the Roman governor. Though removed from us in space and time and set down in a foreign milieu, both the person and the story of Jesus are within the range of our comprehension. Jesus is a figure who belongs to us as part of our history.

But there is another side to the Biblical witness. Jesus does and says things that are strange even to those who approach the narrative prepared to believe. He casts out demons, who cry out when He approaches the one possessed. He performs feats known as miracles, which astonish and startle people around Him. He lives a celibate life in the manner of the Old Testament prophets. He, in fact, claims to be the fulfillment of Old Testament prophecy and that with His appearance the kingdom of God has come. He demands that His followers give up all for His sake and then says: "Whoever confesses publicly that he belongs to Me, I will do the same for him before My Father in heaven. But whoever denies publicly that he belongs to Me, then I will deny him before My Father in heaven" (Matt. 10:32-33 TEV). Strange things happen to Him: Heavenly messengers attend what is said to be His miraculous birth, a voice is heard at His baptism, He is transfigured before His disciples on a mountain. His story ends after He is reported to have been raised from the dead following His crucifixion and seen alive by His followers.

What manner of man was this? For the early church the strange and uncanny elements in the life of Jesus indicated that He was one in whom the eternal God was active in a unique and special way for the salvation of mankind. Today such features in the story of Jesus are often dismissed as legends that grew around His memory in the decades following His death. The real Jesus was something different, they say. The fact is, however, that the early church's witness to Jesus is entirely consistent. Whether early or late, in narrative or discourse, the church's testimony is that Jesus was a man who shared in the life of God and God in His. We are not here discussing whether this is true. Our concern is to make clear what Christians mean when they say that Jesus is "divine" and what the creed intends when it says that Jesus is "Very God of Very God." Both terms assert the Biblical conviction that God was uniquely and redemptively active in the life of Jesus of Nazareth. This, let me emphasize, does not exhaust what Christians mean by Christ's divinity, but it represents a large portion of what it is we as Christians are to accept about Jesus. It can serve as a working definition of the doctrine we are discussing.

"Accepting" Christ

I have used the word *accept* since that is the one most often used in connection with Christian doctrine. But *accept* can make it sound as if faith were something one has to force himself to yield to against his will. Such an understanding is wrong. If true, faith would then become some sort of intellectual condition for membership in the Christian church rather than a spontaneous trust in the love of God. Yet we can understand why people take this view. They hear the word *accept* negatively because of the frequently used statement "You have to accept Christ as the Son of God to be a Christian," or words to that effect.

Perhaps it is the preceding "have to" rather than "accept" that is the trouble here. Whatever it is, we need to emphasize that Christian faith is not "having to accept" anything. This does not mean that you can make of Jesus anything you want and remain in touch with the Biblical witness. It means rather that as soon as you understand the Christian testimony to Jesus as a demand rather than an offer, you have not really understood it at all. When Christians proclaim Christ more like a command than an invitation, they show they have not understood their own Gospel. The early Christians never approached their Jewish and Gentile contemporaries with an order to "accept" Jesus Christ or certain ideas about Him, even the one that He is divine. They offered their fellows a share in the love of God for mankind, and that was Jesus Christ as far as they were concerned. To talk of "having to accept" Christ would have struck the New Testament Christian as odd. The free and living relationship with God, which is what faith is, has nothing to do with compulsion. The nonbeliever has a right to protest when someone in the church tries to brainwash him into saying something he does not honestly believe. The believer has a right to protest when the nonbeliever persists in confusing a confession to Christ with some sort of violation of his integrity as a person.

Ideas of Divinity

It is curious that many people who report difficulty with the doctrine of Christ's divinity assume that they know something — often it appears a great deal — about God. "I believe in God, but I can't accept what the church says about Jesus." What the speaker says is that he knows enough about God and about what constitutes divinity to make a judgment about Jesus Christ. It is a strange stance for an age that claims God is dead! Again and again, in reply, Christians have pointed out what Daniel Jenkins says: "Our answer to the question, 'What think ye of Christ?' is not determined by our answer to the prior question, 'Do you believe there is a God?' The evidence provided by Jesus himself is our chief source for making up our minds whether God exists or not,"[1] and, we would add, for determining what kind of God He in fact is. Jesus baffles us, but at least He is one whom we can imagine, one about whom we have solid evidence in history. Even the Roman historians mention Him. *God* is the ultimate mystery. Christians learn to talk about Him on the basis of His revelation in Jesus Christ. The data on divinity are shaped by Jesus Christ and not developed in isolation from Him. People may believe that they are talking about God apart from Jesus, but when they are speaking about God they often unconsciously presuppose a great deal of what Jesus reveals about Him. Without Christ they would not be able to carry on the debate.

What people frequently look for when they claim to believe in God but not in Christ is some sort of unambiguous proof of Christ's divinity on the order of a miracle. Miracles have been called "faith's most cherished child." They represent the ultimate evidence for divinity. It is well known that the New Testament includes numerous narratives in which Christ performs a miracle. For a certain type of believer the existence of such accounts alone "proves" that Jesus was divine. For the doubter, of course, they do nothing of the kind. He can invent a hundred explanations of a purely natural sort for every miracle story in the Gospels. After reading each account, he still asks for proof.

According to the sources, Jesus never acceded

to the request that He prove His divine mission or origin during His ministry. Whenever He was challenged to give evidence for His claim, He refused, as in the following excerpt:

> Some Pharisees and Sadducees came to Jesus. They wanted to trap Him, so they asked Him to perform a miracle for them, to show God's approval. . . . "How evil and godless are the people of this day!" Jesus added. "You ask Me for a miracle? No! The only miracle you will be given is the miracle of Jonah." So He left them and went away. (Matt. 16:1, 4 TEV)

The enigmatic offer of the "miracle of Jonah" is typical of the way Jesus spoke of Himself and His mission. He frequently alludes to the Old Testament, here to forecast His resurrection. Jesus counted on the impact of His message and deeds to awaken trust in Him, not on anything that would be taken for magic. His divinity was not to be demonstrated in power but in the love of a gracious and forgiving God, which He conveyed to men. His presence was God's offer of fellowship. To prove that this was so would destroy what was being offered, for love that has to be proved is love that is not received.

God Hidden and Revealed

In the chapter entitled "Thinking About Faith" I suggested an additional reason why God's presence and activity in Jesus Christ cannot be proved in the ordinary sense of the word. The New Testament sees Jesus as the ultimate revelation of God. To reveal means to uncover, to make known what has been secret, to allow what was hidden to appear. The God of the Bible is one who reveals Himself, but never in a way that totally exposes Him to men. There is always an aspect of hiddenness to God's revelation of Himself, always something that keeps Him beyond the full reach of man's gaze. We are never compelled to acknowledge God's presence or activity. The men of the Bible constantly had to decide whether they were dealing with God. Sometimes they had the help of a "sign," but the sign was never the proof that moderns would be satisfied with or require.

If Jesus is in fact the ultimate revelation of God (cf. Hebrews 1:1-2), we would expect His appearance to be qualitatively the same as revelation elsewhere in the Bible. That is to say, we would expect God to be both hidden and revealed in Him—hidden to those who desire God to relieve them of the necessity for faith, revealed to those who are willing to allow God the freedom to disclose Himself as He wills and take no offense at it. In a way similar to God's revelation in the Old Testament, Jesus offers men "signs" that God is with Him, but the signs are never unambiguous. This is the reason Jesus' contemporaries have no advantage over us in coming to faith, for there never was a time when people were exempt from faith when it came to grasping the mystery of Jesus' person. It was possible even for those who saw Him cast out demons to theorize that He possessed His power because He was in alliance with the prince of demons. Others believed that He did so by the finger of God and sensed that the kingdom of God was coming upon them.

The Way to Christ

Who then has access to the mystery of Christ? Jesus Himself tells us: "Come to Me, all who labor and are heavy laden, and I will give you rest." Again, "I came not to call the righteous, but sinners." One can understand what is meant by the divinity of Christ only when he is aware of his need for the forgiving grace of God. We today should understand our need for forgiveness better than previous generations. Because of modern methods of communication like television, each of us is an eyewitness to the wars, assassinations, and riots that plague our era and for which we are individually responsible. He who recognizes this guilt as his is a step closer to desiring its forgiveness. To such a person the claim of Christ comes not as the wild assertion of some madman or faker, or as the impossible imaginings of a group of deluded disciples, but as *truth*. In Jesus is heard *God's* word of forgiveness, and for that reason we place Jesus on the side of God.⟩

There is a tendency in all of us to reject the Bible's testimony to Jesus as too complicated and mysterious. We prefer something or someone simpler than Jesus Christ, who is true God and yet a real human person in whom God acts redemptively. That forces us to acknowledge Christ as Someone special. The desire for simplicity is the root cause of all estimates of Jesus that fall short of the full Biblical testimony. Yet, what in all nature and history is not in the last analysis mysteriously complex? What is more baffling than the riddle of an existence caught in the conflict between good and evil? As the popular song has it:

If the soul is darkened by a fear it cannot name,
If the mind is baffled when the rules don't fit
the game,

Who will answer? Who will answer? Who will answer?

Hallelujah! Hallelujah! Hallelujah! [2]

Without a divine Christ in whom the living God is present and active and who is "Very God of Very God," there would be no one to answer. A simple, uncomplicated "Christ" who coins phrases and teaches universal truths and at last dies for his convictions can be admired perhaps, but in the end is irrelevant. He tells us nothing we could not tell ourselves. And if that is all Christ was, it is difficult to imagine why anyone would bother to crucify Him — or die for Him afterwards. But a Christ who is something different, something that human history could not produce on its own, is indeed "another matter." He can create hope and lead us to affirm life as a gift rather than a curse. The mystery of an existence beset by evil, and the mystery of our guilt, are met and overcome by a greater mystery, the mystery of God's gracious and forgiving love in Jesus of Nazareth.

Hallelujah! Hallelujah! Hallelujah!

What I am saying is that to believe in Christ you have to see Him whole. Many people begin their consideration of Jesus by investigating the details of His life: His birth, His miracles, His trial and death. That is like walking up to a mural and staring at one detail of the artist's work. What we need to do is step back and view the whole picture, the human condition and Christ's relation to it. Better, we need to begin with *our* condition and consider Christ in reference to ourselves. The divinity of Christ is not a subject for religiously inclined people to discuss in polite after-dinner conversations over a good cordial, or for college students to debate at conferences. Jesus Christ is God's offer of hope to us when we become aware of the dark and hostile powers that bear upon us in this world. Those who allow Christ to touch them will discover what it means to say that He is divine.

6
THE NEW FREEDOM AND THE HOLY SPIRIT

YEARS AGO the University of Massachusetts had a tradition known as Spring Day. On some especially beautiful May morning, one of the students would climb Old Chapel's tower and ring the bells. Everyone would then take the day off for an impromptu vacation.

Spring Day was a delightful institution until it degenerated into something less than the enjoyment of the great outdoors. When activities became too wild, the administration abolished the day, presumably forever. The student newspaper, however, kept the memory of Spring Day alive and, of course, campaigned for its revival. Finally someone climbed the tower a few years ago and rang the bells again. Only a small percentage of the student body took off for the (now illegal) holiday, but those who did outdistanced previous generations in the intensity of their revels. The invention of electronic musical instruments and the increase in the number of available automobiles for transporting beer and girls added new dimensions to the exercises. At last report authorities of both town and gown have acted to quell any further revivals of the tradition.

Spring Day by itself is a matter of little consequence. Adult society exceeds it many times, both in crudity and pointlessness. But the day is important as a symbol of one of the changes that have taken place in our society with respect to morals and behavior. While nonparticipants privately derided what went on, it is significant that there was an almost total absence of anything like public indignation aimed at the revelers. Everyone on campus understood that there would be nothing of the kind, which meant that each person was free to make the decision to participate or not on his own. To join or not to join was the question of the day, but it was a question that each individual faced without fear of social ostracism. The consequence of joining the party might have been a lower mark because of a lecture that was missed, or some other self-inflicted penalty. The student body, however, had no sanctions that it could (or desired to) impose on those of its number who left campus that day.

The New Freedom

Without realizing it, perhaps, students at the University of Massachusetts reflected the fact that America and a large part of the Western world have entered the era of the permissive society, the time of the new freedom. Until fairly recently, Western morality was controlled by conventions that operated both as a brake and a guide for personal behavior. Public disapproval of deviations from accepted norms expressed itself in painful and frightening reprisals. (Think of Hester Prymme's punishment in *The Scarlet Letter*.) Modern society has lost interest in enforcing personal behavior patterns and to a large extent has become morally neutral. What consenting adults do among themselves is more and more regarded as their business. The individual may do with his private life what he wishes as long as he does not invade the rights of others or threaten them with injury. There are still some controversial areas in which the question of the public interest is not clear, such as homosexual practices and the use of certain narcotics, but there is no mistaking the trend. Society is moving toward greater personal freedom rather than less, as the appearance of the hippies testifies. Mass media both reflect and encourage the new freedom. It will soon be difficult to boast, "A few years ago this picture could not have been made."

Naturally there are many who wring their hands over the moral neutrality of society and the enthusiasm with which it is being greeted by the young. People have always worried about the way youth were turning out, but we are the first to speak expressly of "the generation gap," which is largely a matter of the relative freedom of the two age groups. Many who view the "decay of morals" with alarm would like to make it impossible for anyone to buy contraceptives or pornographic literature or pot, or failing that, to use them. The attempt is as futile as trying to get some youth to cut their hair. There must be limits to personal behavior — "dikes against lovelessness," as Bishop J. A. T. Robinson termed them — that each society has to erect, although it is not easy to say where and what kind they shall be. What is clear is that we shall never succeed in reintroducing the moral conventions of, say, 1869.

Sociologists assert that many factors combined to produce the changes in societal attitudes toward personal behavior. Population growth and increased urbanization have generated a mobile, impersonal, anonymous life-style that makes enforcement of moral codes difficult. Secularization has resulted in "the death of God" and given rise to a nonjudgmental view of private behavior, free of censure or praise. As Jim Casey says in *The Grapes of Wrath*, "There ain't no sin and there ain't no virtue. There's just stuff people do." Such a point of view hardly provides the jumping-off point for moral crusades. Instead of worrying about the "stuff people do," modern society, especially youth, interests itself far more in problems pertaining to poverty, racial justice, and peace. While the ghettos seethe and the country's underprivileged are not adequately provided for, no congressman would dream of introducing a bill to revive prohibition or to regulate the nationwide distribution of contraceptives. We have experienced a radical reshuffling of our national moral priorities since Colonial and Victorian days.

The church too has done some reshuffling. Modern-day Christians believe the desire for freedom can be good and of real spiritual worth. Christians today often demonstrate that they understand that faith means more than observing rules. It was a gain when some of the stultifying restrictions that inhibited personal expression dropped away. Mature Christian individuals are persons who should fully be themselves. Along with the realization that Christian faith is more than an external conforming to what is regarded as morality has come the conviction that life in Christ relates to the social as well as the personal order. We now recognize, for example, that sex is not the main area in which a person can fall into grievous sin. It is, sadly, easier to remain sexually pure than to remain free of the racism in American society. *Obscenity* is a word that has been enlarged to include any type of debasing behavior, from the neglect of the poor and the mistreatment of welfare recipients to the callousness of the military in its choice of tactics to fight limited wars.

Freedom is a great experience, but it poses problems. How do you personally know what is right or wrong under given circumstances? Where do you go for guidance in the choice of values in a permissive society? What do you have to fall back on for inner strength to maintain your values at a time when anything goes? Many articles have been written charging America with a loss of moral standards and a corruption of will, but few offer any practical guidelines or alternatives for the concerned individual. Some writers content themselves with a call for a return to "the old paths wherein is the good way," by which they mean traditional Judeo-Christian ethics as interpreted by 19th-century Protestantism. Advocates of return argue that morality does not change because human beings do not change. What is right now has always been right and always will be right. Other voices call for a "new morality" in which each ethical situation is to be viewed as unique and in which decisions are made individually on the basis of love alone. These hold that Jesus protested against the rigid legalism of the Pharisees, who tried to make love into a set of rules. Far from inspiring obedience, they say, legalism leads to slavery and in the end incites people to rebellion. Meanwhile youth has been forging a do-it-yourself ethic that places heavy emphasis on "doing your own thing" and on the three virtues of love, friendship, and peace.

Both the "code ethicists," as James A. Pike calls them,[1] and proponents of the new morality sincerely aim at helping people answer the question, What shall I do? *But this is where their weakness lies.* The question facing people today is not simply that of ethical choice, perplexing and insistent as that may be. Before we can discriminate between competing ethical claims or choose one course of action over another, we have to answer the prior question, What are we as human beings? We have to begin farther back, so to speak, and look at the actor rather than the action. It stands to reason that to *do* right we must *be* right. When we consider the actor, the problem of ethical decision in the time of the new freedom assumes a different dimension and becomes the problem of human nature.

The Bondage of the Will

The struggle with the self has received many literary expressions, of which none is more poignant than that by J. D. Salinger in *The Catcher in the Rye.* Sixteen-year-old Holden Caulfield has come to New York from prep school and taken a room in a hotel. One of the first things he observes is a man and a woman in a drunken orgy squirting water over each other. He confesses to himself, ''That kind of junk is sort of fascinating to watch, even if you don't want it to be.'' He laments, ''It's really too bad that so much crumby stuff is a lot of fun sometimes.'' The incident leads him to some further conclusions:

> I keep making up these sex rules for myself, and then I break them right away. Last year I made a rule that I was going to quit horsing around with girls . . . . I broke it, though, the same week I made it—the same *night,* as a matter of fact. I spent the whole night necking with a terrible phony named Anne Louise Sherman. Sex is something I just don't understand.[2]

Holden clearly knows what kind of ethical standards he wishes to maintain. No code ethicist could spell it out plainer. He is, however, honest enough to recognize his inability to carry out his resolves and admits his failure to himself. Furthermore, he recognizes what many idealistic young people today overlook: "So much crumby stuff is a lot of fun sometimes." In trying to act rightly, we face the problem of the powerful attraction evil has for us along with the difficulty of knowing exactly what to do.

There is a remarkable parallel between Holden's confession and the statement of St. Paul:

> I can will what is right, but I cannot do it. For I do not do the good I want, but the evil I do not want is what I do. . . . So I find it to be a law that when I want to do right, evil lies close at hand. (Rom. 7:18-19, 21 RSV)

When he reaches this point, Paul cries out: "Wretched man that I am! Who will deliver me from this body of death?" He answers his own question: "Thanks be to God through Jesus Christ our Lord!" (Vv. 24-25)

The Gift of the Spirit

Paul saw that the ethical problem is more than *knowing* what to do. He knew the standard of God's law as expressed in the commandments: God created man to love Him above all, and to love the neighbor as himself. Man as he was supposed to be, so Paul knew, was one who obeyed God and lived to serve the neighbor in love. He tried to reach that level of righteousness in the keeping of God's law. But his knowledge of what he ought to be and his determination to be that kind of person were not enough. He realized he needed the power to destroy the dismal cycle of making and breaking resolutions in his ethical struggle. To do right, he needed help from outside himself, something new that would reshape his life. For Paul that something new was the Spirit of Jesus Christ he received when he came to faith.

One of the brightest hopes entertained by Israel during the Old Testament period pertained to a general outpouring of the Spirit so that men might know God and be able to do His will. Paul, along with the early church, saw that hope fulfilled in Jesus Christ. Along with faith in Christ believers received the energizing, life-transforming Spirit. When a man had the Spirit of Jesus (and that is what made him a Christian, according to Romans 8:9 and other New Testament texts), he was alive to God and had been given the energy to break loose from old habits and attitudes. His new relationship to God gave him a "feel" for the right. What Christians today need first, Paul would argue, is not more Law instruction but the new Spirit, the Spirit of Christ. This they can have as a gift from God, who is ready to give to those willing to receive.

It is hard to exaggerate the importance the Spirit had for the early church. The New Testament writers use an amazingly rich variety of expressions to designate the "fruits" of the Spirit. But if we had to summarize in one word what the experience of the Spirit of Jesus meant for the earliest believers, we would not be wrong in using the word *freedom*. St. Paul writes, "Where the Spirit of the Lord is, there is freedom" (2 Cor. 3:17 RSV), and that is no accident. As Paul van Buren has pointed out,[3] freedom was the characteristic life-style of Jesus in His days on earth. His sovereign freedom shines through every parable, saying, or incident in the four gospels. He always knew what had to be done and was never constrained by fear or favor to leave it undone. No legal restrictions ever kept Him from fulfilling what His Father commanded. He was bound by no false ties of family. He did not worry about safety or reputation. The point of the miracle stories is that even the laws of nature were unable to contain Him: He was Lord of the wind and the sea. His freedom was absolute. This is the reason why the common people were attracted to Him. This is what impressed them so powerfully.

Jesus' teaching reveals that He wishes the same kind of freedom for His followers. He wants them to be delivered of any anxiety over law or safety or guilt of sin. Nothing should leave them "up tight." But the freedom Jesus exhibited and communicated was entirely positive in character. It was a freedom from every type of bondage to enable men to serve God and the neighbor. Jesus did not employ His liberty for selfish advantage, but used it to minister and to give His life finally "as a ransom for many." In the same Spirit Jesus liberates from moralism, legalism, and selfish restrictions for service. Jesus promised that He would make those who followed Him truly free. That promise is kept when they receive the Spirit by which they are enabled to love.

For people living in the era of the new freedom the New Testament offers not "old morality" but something in tune with the times—liberty in the Spirit of Jesus. That means, by the way, that we do not use Paul or any other New Testament writer properly if we unimaginatively transfer the advice given to first-century Christians into our times and try to use it as a guide. We have to get behind what is said and ground ethics on the New Testament's foundation, the Spirit of Jesus. Each ethical situation becomes a call to Christians to re-call what they have received as new creatures in Christ. In a way the "new morality" people are correct: God's morality is always a new morality, a fresh creation of the Spirit working on our contradictory natures and leading us to a new experience of freedom to fulfill His purpose for men.

Finding the Answers

If we follow Paul and seek to share in the Spirit of Jesus, we have a unique resource for dealing with our contemporary ethical confusion. By means of the Spirit we can "home in" on the answers required of us. At first such daring might seem frightening. Many people are afraid to leave the safe confines of rules and regulations, of codes and prescriptions. Freedom seems inevitably to turn into license or pure subjectivity. Life in the Spirit is indeed a kind of "look, Ma, no hands" existence, but it is never without control or direction. The beautiful thing about life in the Spirit of Christ is that it combines liberty with responsibility. "Love and do what you like," said St. Augustine long ago. We would say: "Live by the Spirit of Christ and do what you like." You will not go wrong. You will leave behind your fears and confusion and be led to serve the neighbor without distracting attention to yourself.

But not even the new creation in the Spirit

automatically answers every question for Christians in the realm of ethics. The Spirit is the context within which we consider ethical decisions and the source of the insights and strength we need to make them, but that does not eliminate the necessity for hard thinking to make the right decisions on many questions we face today. In the modern world few ethical problems are easy. Most are extremely complicated because of such new factors as population growth and advances in technology. Abortion, divorce, the problem of selective conscientious objection, business ethics, international relations, and most pressing of all, decisions in the area of medicine and human engineering—all these are highly complex issues that cannot be answered in a simplistic or lazy manner. Sluggishness is not what decision-making in the Spirit means. What the Bible says about life in the Spirit encourages us to use all technical resources available in determining our action and confer with those who share the Spirit with us in arriving at ethical guidelines for our times. The burden of responding to both simple and complicated questions is not to be carried by the individual alone. Others share it with us. The church is meant to be a fellowship where we can obtain inspiration and guidance for our performance of God's will in the world.

The Church

I realize that for many people, particularly young adults, the church is an anachronism, something straight out of the Middle Ages. The building with a tower to which people come to hear a man talk on Sundays and the enterprise behind it simply do not fit in with modern life. But if the building houses people who are sincerely seeking answers to the burning issues of the day and the power to change things, the church might be more relevant than the detractors imagine. Of course, congregations may fail at being Spirit-led communities that help people to love. They are made up of frail human beings —people like you and me. But a surprising number are what they were intended to be, and the possibility of renewal exists for the rest. The church experiences the living presence of Jesus as the Word about Him is shared and His sacraments are celebrated. These are the means through which the Spirit comes to people, says the New Testament. People receive the Spirit of Jesus when they participate in the life of His community. "Going to church" often is thought to be dull, boring, uninteresting, and as something to turn people off. But if the Spirit has His way, worship is a lively "happening" in which people come to a greater experience of love and freedom.

It is popular these days to cite all kinds of statistics to show how religion is losing ground in our culture. Figures point to a decline in church membership. Many people are beginning to think it odd that Christians continue to worship, pray, commune, and serve in the name of Jesus Christ. Here again we see what it means to enjoy freedom. If Christians were to depend on the approval of society for their faith and mission, the present position of the church might be considered as threatened. But Christians are free from the need for such approval, since they know themselves to stand under God's love in Jesus Christ. They have been liberated to concentrate on ways in which God would have them serve in today's world. Some things can safely be left in God's hand. The relative position of the church with regard to other institutions in society is one of them. If you stop to think about it, a minority position for the church in the world, if it is to be, might be exhilarating. It could be that such a church would be more responsive to the Spirit than ever.

For Christians this is a great time to be alive. Fewer and fewer voices telling us what to do opens the way for a greater awareness of who we are in the Spirit, who creates genuine freedom. The new freedom of today's society allows us to display the authentic life-style of the Christian, which is liberty — not the false liberty of those who succumb again to the bondage of self or society but real liberty of love in Jesus Christ. "Where the Spirit of the Lord is, there is freedom."

Notes

CHAPTER 1

1. Gabriel Vahanian, *The Death of God* (New York: George Braziller, 1961), p. 188.
2. Friedrich Nietzsche, *Ecce Homo,* in *The Philosophy of Nietzsche,* ed. Clifton Fadiman (New York: The Modern Library, 1927), p. 932.
3. Dietrich Bonhoeffer, *Letters and Papers from Prison,* ed. Eberhard Bethge (New York: The Macmillan Company, 1953), p. 165.
4. Ibid.
5. Martin Buber, *The Eclipse of God* (New York: Harper & Row, 1952), p. 73.
6. Abraham Joshua Heschel, *God in Search of Man* (New York: Harper & Row, 1955), p. 169.

CHAPTER 2

1. Ingmar Bergman, "The Seventh Seal," in *Four Screen Plays of Ingmar Bergman* (New York: Simon and Schuster, 1960), p. 111.
2. Abraham Joshua Heschel, *God in Search of Man* (New York: Harper & Row, 1955), pp. 74—75 and *passim.*
3. See the essay by Robert Johann, S. J., "Knowledge, Commitment, and the Real," in *Wisdom in Depth,* ed. Vincent F. Daues, S. J., et al. (Milwaukee: Bruce Publishing Company, 1966). Also, Carl Michalson, *The Rationality of Faith* (New York: Charles Scribner's Sons, 1963), pp. 36 ff., where Michalson discusses the theories of Michael Polanyi and Ernst Cassirer. Polanyi holds that "objective detachment is a myth," according to Michalson.
4. Fredrick Buechner has a delightful section in his book *The Magnificent Defeat* (Greenwich: Seabury

Press, 1966) in which he speculates on what man's reaction would be were God to reveal Himself in a visible way; cf. "Message in the Stars," pp. 44 ff.

5. John Updike, *Pigeon Feathers and Other Stories* (New York: Fawcett World Library, 1963), p. 92.

CHAPTER 3

1. M. Holmes Hartshorne, *The Faith to Doubt* (Englewood Cliffs: Prentice-Hall, Inc., 1963), p. 1.

2. © Copyright 1935 by Gershwin Publishing Corporation. Copyright renewed. Used by permission of Chappell & Co., Inc.

3. The noted Harvard psychologist, Gordon Allport, makes a perceptive comment on the tendency of students to reject that which they have not fully considered. In *The Individual and His Religion* (New York: The Macmillan Company, 1950), he says:

> There remains one aspect of the loss of theocentric faith and the drift to non-theological liberalism to be considered. The shift is unquestionably due in part, though not entirely, to the ignorance of students today regarding the teachings of theology. The "queen of sciences" has fallen from her throne. . . . One may read student autobiographies dealing with personal religious history without finding the slightest comprehension of the theological position which they, more likely than not, are in the process of rejecting. . . . They know next to nothing of St. Thomas Aquinas, Meister Eckhardt, Luther, Calvin, Wesley, Swedenborg, Kierkegaard, Newman, Tyrrell, Ritschl, Barth, Bowne, Niebuhr, or any other of the brilliant minds who have wrestled with the rational aspects of the Christian faith. These thinkers are no less aware than the critical undergraduate

of today of the intellectual difficulties involved, and of the degree to which institutional religion falls short of its professions. The positions they have achieved are hard won, and possibly valid for themselves alone. But their efforts, none-theless, might serve as models of the strenuous thinking demanded of every aspirant seeking religious maturity. (P. 46)

4. Quoted by Hartshorne, p. 11.
5. Albert Camus, *The Stranger* (New York: Alfred A. Knopf, Inc., 1959), pp. 145 ff.

CHAPTER 4

1. Rolf Hochhuth, *The Deputy* (New York: Grove Press, Inc., 1964), Act Five, Scene Two, p. 246.
2. Archibald MacLeish, *JB* (Cambridge: The Riverside Press, 1956), The Prologue, p. 11.
3. Richard Luecke, *New Meanings for New Beings* (Philadelphia: Fortress Press, 1964), p. 30.
4. John Updike, *Rabbit, Run* (New York: Fawcett World Library, 1968), p. 230.
5. From the play *The Sign of Jonah,* by Guenter Rutenborn, published by Thomas Nelson & Sons. With the permission of the author's agent, Kurt Hellmer, 52 Vanderbilt Ave., New York, N. Y. 10017.
6. Dietrich Bonhoeffer, *Letters and Papers from Prison,* ed. Eberhard Bethge (New York: The Macmillan Company, 1953), pp. 219—220.
7. As quoted by C. F. D. Moule in *The Sacrifice of Christ* (Philadelphia: Fortress Press, 1964), p. 25.

CHAPTER 5

1. Daniel Jenkins, *The Christian Belief in God* (Philadelphia: The Westminster Press, 1964), p. 25.
2. © Copyright 1957 by L. E. Aute. Ediciones Musicales RCA Espanola, S. A. All rights for the U. S. A.

controlled by Sunbury Music, Inc., 1133 Avenue of the Americas, New York, N. Y. 10036. Reprinted by Permission of Sunbury Music, Inc.

CHAPTER 6

1. James A. Pike, *You and the New Morality* (New York: Harper & Row, 1967), pp. 4—5.
2. J. D. Salinger, *The Catcher in the Rye* (New York: The New American Library of World Literature, 1960), p. 58.
3. Paul M. van Buren, *The Secular Meaning of the Gospel* (New York: The Macmillan Company, 1963), pp. 123 ff.